# The National Archives

# The National Archives

## R. Conrad Stein

**Franklin Watts**
A Division of Scholastic Inc.
New York • Toronto • London • Auckland • Sydney
Mexico City • New Delhi • Hong Kong
Danbury, Connecticut

**Note to readers:** Definitions for words in **bold** can be found in the Glossary at the back of this book.

The photograph on the cover shows Exhibit Hall at the National Archives Building in Washington, D.C. The photograph opposite the title page shows the front of the National Archives Building in late afternoon.

Photographs © 2002: Art Resource, NY/National Portrait Gallery, Smithsonian Institution: 16; Bridgeman Art Library International Ltd., London/New York: 45 (National Archives Trust); Corbis Images: 26; Folio, Inc.: 2 (Walter Bibikow), 42 (Rick Buettner), 48 (Catherine Karnow), 28 (John W. Keith), cover (Pete Souza); Hulton Archive/Getty Images: 46 (Mathew B. Brady), 53; Jonathan Wallen: 5 left, 5 right, 14, 18, 30, 31, 38, 41, 44; National Archives and Records Administration: 20, 21, 22, 47 (PhotoAssist), 8, 9, 11, 34; North Wind Picture Archives: 6, 17; Photri Inc.: 35, 36, 43; Richard T. Nowitz: 13, 32, 33; Superstock, Inc.: 10.

**Library of Congress Cataloging-in-Publication Data**

Stein, R. Conrad.
    The National Archives / R. Conrad Stein.
        p. cm. — (Watts library)
    Includes bibliographical references and index.
    Summary: Looks at the history and work of the National Archives, where original documents, photographs, and other important materials are stored.
    ISBN 0-531-12032-5 (lib. bdg.)   0-531-16602-3 (pbk.)
    1. Archives—United States. 2. United States. National Archives and Records Administration.
[1. United States. National Archives and Records Administration.] I. Title. II. Series.

CD3023 .S74 2002
027.5'0973—dc21
                                                  2001007141

# Contents

Thomas Jefferson leaned over his desk as he drafted the Declaration of Independence, a defiant document that changed the course of history.

# Chapter One

# A Look at the National Archives

Thomas Jefferson had the habit of writing while standing up instead of sitting. In June 1776, he crouched over a desk in Philadelphia and wrote one of the most honored documents in American history: the Declaration of Independence. In elegant, forceful language, the declaration announced to the world that the thirteen English colonies had broken away from

*This mural,* The Declaration of Independence *by Barry Faulkner, is displayed above the original document at the National Archives Building in Washington, D.C. In the painting, Jefferson presents the Declaration of Independence to the Continental Congress in 1776. All twenty-eight delegates stand around him.*

their mother country and had burst forth as the new and independent United States.

The original handwritten Declaration of Independence is now displayed at the National Archives Building in Washington, D.C. Above the document is a huge mural showing Jefferson as he presents the declaration to John Hancock and other leaders of the American independence movement. The painting captures a dramatic moment in the lives of these patriots. In the eyes of King George III of England, the Declaration of Independence represented an act of treason punishable by hanging.

James Madison, another American founding father, studied many different forms of government. He was especially

interested in the political organization of the Iroquois Indians, a group of native tribes living in New York State. Madison admired the Iroquois **confederation**, a system in which member tribes had a certain degree of self-rule while overall power went to the central government. In 1787, Madison served as the major author of the U.S. Constitution, which created a confederation system for the United States. Some historians believe that Madison based the new government's structure on the Iroquois model.

The original Constitution, handwritten on parchment, now stands in the National Archives alongside the Declaration of Independence. Above the Constitution is another mural showing James Madison presenting the document to George Washington and other statesmen. Both the Declaration of Independence and the Constitution murals were painted in 1936 by artist Barry Faulkner.

On December 15, 1791, the first ten **amendments** (changes or additions) were incorporated into the Constitution. These ten amendments are collectively called the Bill of Rights. They prevent the federal government from limiting fundamental individual liberties, such as freedom of speech and

**Meet Mr. Madison**

James Madison (1751–1836) was the fourth U.S. president, serving from 1809 to 1817. In 1810, President Madison signed a congressional act aimed at improving the storage of government papers. This act was one of the first steps in the creation of the National Archives.

freedom of worship. The original Bill of Rights is also displayed at the National Archives.

These three honored items—the Declaration of Independence, the Constitution, and the Bill of Rights—are called the Charters of Freedom. More than any other documents, they are the cornerstones of American liberty. The charters are priceless, fragile, and almost holy to the nation. They stand secure and preserved in the National Archives, a treasure trove of American history.

## America's Closet

The National Archives Building sits in the heart of Washington, D.C. The Charters of Freedom are displayed in a section called Exhibit Hall. More than one million visitors enter this

The United States Constitution was handwritten on parchment. Pictured here is page one, displayed near the Declaration of Independence at the National Archives.

hall each year. The rest of the building is a huge storehouse enclosing 80,000 cubic feet (23,000 cubic meters) of space. Its libraries' shelves and airtight vaults contain official papers, maps, and many other objects.

Many of the documents at the National Archives played a glorious role in the American story. For example, the Emancipation Proclamation, the first step that the United States took to free its slaves, is stored there. So, too, is the Nineteenth Amendment to the Constitution, which gave women the right to vote when it was adopted in 1920.

The National Archives also holds reminders of shameful chapters in American history. For example, its libraries hold manifests (cargo lists) of slave ships that once brought Africans to the New World in chains. Also in the archives is the presidential order that sent some 100,000 Japanese Americans to internment camps during World War II (1939–1945).

The National Archives could be called America's closet. It is the place where the nation stores old keepsakes in much the way that a family saves high-school diplomas, photo albums,

## What's in a Word?

The word *archive* dates back to the ancient Greek word *arkhein,* translated as "the original" or "the first one." An archive is a place where historical relics and original documents, such as the Declaration of Independence, are preserved and protected. Many other countries have their own archives. The National Archives of the United States is the world's most modern archives facility.

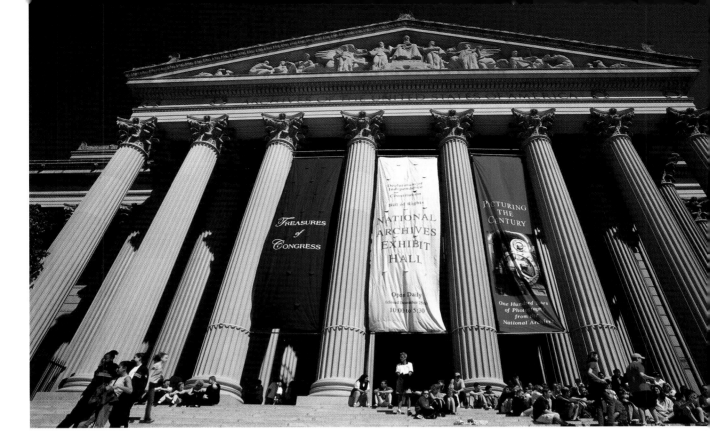

and other **memorabilia**. The archives serves as both a museum and a working library. Court records, treaties, presidential proclamations, and other documents are there to be studied. Also present are more than 14 million photographs, 300,000 reels of motion pictures, and about 200,000 sound recordings. In all, the National Archives holds almost one billion items—and therefore has a billion stories to tell.

*More than one million people visit Exhibit Hall at the National Archives Building every year. This picture was taken on a bright spring day.*

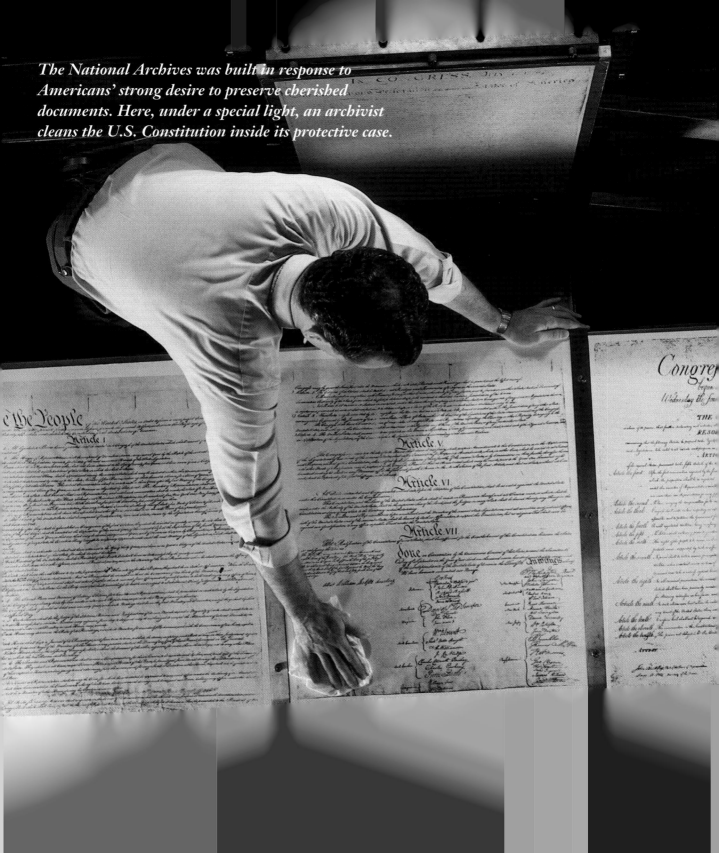

The National Archives was built in response to
Americans' strong desire to preserve cherished
documents. Here, under a special light, an archivist
cleans the U.S. Constitution inside its protective case.

# Chapter Two

# A Dream Fulfilled

How did the National Archives, this amazing storehouse of **Americana**, come into being? It all began with Americans' wish to preserve official papers and other objects that served as milestones in their progress as a nation. The desire to protect cherished items dates back to the earliest days of American history.

Almost two hundred years ago, Thomas Jefferson warned his fellow citizens, "Time and accident are committing daily havoc on the originals deposited in

## America's First Archivist

Charles Thomson (1729–1824) was a schoolmaster and a widely respected scholar. In 1774, he was made the official secretary of the Continental Congress, charged with the duty of keeping and preserving records. Thus Thomson is regarded as the nation's first archivist.

our public offices." When he wrote these words, Jefferson might have been looking at his own Declaration of Independence. Even during his lifetime, the document had yellowed, and the words had begun to fade.

Before the National Archives was established, many of the nation's precious papers suffered from neglect. For decades, each department of government kept its own documents and records. Some of these agencies stacked records under leaky roofs, where dampness and mold destroyed the paper. In addition, fires frequently broke out in Washington during the 1800s, and thousands of irreplaceable papers were lost as buildings went up in flames.

As early as the 1830s, President Andrew Jackson (1767–1845) declared the need for "a fireproof building [to hold the nation's] important books and papers." Despite Jackson's

## Rough Road for the Declaration

During the War of 1812, the Declaration of Independence was hurriedly stuffed into a linen bag, taken by horse-drawn cart from Washington, D.C., and hidden overnight in a gristmill in Virginia. The next day, it was moved to a private home in Leesburg, Virginia. Quick action was essential, for just hours later, a British army regiment marched into Washington and burned many public buildings, including the White House. For thirty-five years, the declaration hung in a frame at the U.S. Patent Office, after which it was moved to the State Department and various other places. It was often exposed to sunlight, which caused the document to fade. Today the handwritten words and signatures on the Declaration of Independence are barely legible.

## Damaged Goods

The 1803 court case *Marbury v. Madison* produced a landmark decision in American history. It established judicial review, the Supreme Court's power to declare an act of Congress unconstitutional. In 1898, several records pertaining to the *Marbury* case were partially destroyed by fire. One is pictured above.

warning, little was done either to erect such a building or to establish an archives office. Meanwhile, precious papers continued to deteriorate or to become lost. In 1921, the Commerce Department was struck by a disastrous fire that damaged records dating back to 1790 and completely destroyed the 1890 census reports. According to a newspaper article written at the time, the census records had been stored on wooden shelves "in ideal conditions for total destruction."

J. Franklin Jameson (1859–1937) was also a strong **advocate** for founding an archives agency. Born in Somerville, Massachusetts, Jameson was one of the nation's leading historians. In the course of his research, he was shocked to see how damaged vital treaties and historic papers had become. Establishing a national archives agency to preserve such records soon became a passion for him. Jameson's efforts were rewarded in 1934, when the National Archives Establishment was made an official agency of the government and Congress provided $8.5 million in funds to construct a National Archives Building. Jameson's dream was finally fulfilled, just three years before his death.

# Building the Temple

A planning committee decided that the new archives building would be located in Washington, D.C., between Seventh and Eighth Streets, with entrances on both Pennsylvania and Constitution Avenues. The location was perfect: midway between the Capitol Building and the White House. Standing on those grounds, however, was a building called Center Market, which had served the capital city for more than a hundred years. For months after Center Market was leveled, nearby streets were flooded with swarming rats that were suddenly made homeless due to the construction. President Herbert Hoover laid the cornerstone for the National Archives Building on February 20, 1933. Hoover said, "This temple of our history will appropriately be one of the most beautiful buildings in America, an expression of the American soul."

In the end, the National Archives Building cost $12 million to build. This figure might seem like a bargain today,

*It took hard work, patience, and $12 million to raise a heavy stone building over the swampy ground of the National Archives Building site. This photograph was taken during construction on November 2, 1933.*

but in the 1930s, it was enormous. It was also more than twice the original estimated price. The committee had not taken into account the swampy land that covered most of the building site. Workers had to drive 8,575 **pilings** into the spongy ground to create a solid foundation for the building. The pilings, as well as other difficulties associated with building a huge structure over wetlands, drove up the cost.

Upon completion in 1935, the National Archives was—and still is—one of the most handsome buildings in Washington. Designed by architect John Russell Pope, the building is true to the neoclassical style. Neoclassical revival architecture is inspired by the grand, many-columned structures of ancient Greece and Rome. Other Washington landmarks, such as the

White House, the Capitol, the Treasury Building, the Jefferson Memorial, and the Lincoln Memorial, were also constructed in the neoclassical tradition.

The National Archives is ringed by seventy-two **Corinthian** columns with delicate, flowerlike carvings gracing their tops. At the main entrance stand two massive bronze doors. Each door weighs 6.5 tons and is 40 feet (12 meters) high, 10 feet (3 m) wide, and 1 foot (30 centimeters) thick.

Inside the National Archives Building are twenty-one stack areas where researchers can work. The building is constructed without windows because even the best-sealed windows can allow outside air to creep in. To properly preserve paper, the air inside has to be kept moisture-free and at a nearly constant temperature. Elaborate fire-safety equipment is in place on every floor. The structure is as airtight and fireproof as any large building on Earth.

# Treasures of the Temple

Archivists and other staff moved into the National Archives Building in November 1935. Items long held by various agencies were at last gathered under one roof. What prizes did the

## Deed to the Past

The National Archives' oldest item concerning American land is a deed giving a planter 12 acres (4.9 hectares) of land in Virginia. The deed was signed in 1678 by Royal Governor Herbert Jeffreys.

## Lieutenant Clark's Map

In 1804, President Jefferson sent explorers Meriweather Lewis and William Clark into the unexplored West to scout out the newly purchased Louisiana Territory. The National Archives holds a map hand-drawn by Clark during his exciting mission of discovery. It is one of some fifteen million maps held by the agency.

National Archives now possess? The list is endless. Following are just a few outstanding historical articles housed at the National Archives.

Treaties made with foreign nations are stepping-stones that trace the growth of the United States. The Louisiana Purchase Treaty (1803) paved the way for President Jefferson to buy the enormous Louisiana Territory from France and, thus, double the size of the United States. The Oregon Treaty, signed with Great Britain in 1846, and the Treaty of Guadalupe Hidalgo, made with Mexico in 1848, completed the young country's journey from sea to sea. All three of these nation-building agreements are stored in the National Archives Building.

The National Archives contains acts of Congress that have shaped the future of the nation. One good example is the Homestead Act, written in 1862, which developed the American West by offering 160 acres (65 ha) of free land to any settler willing to establish a farm and maintain it for five years. Other congressional acts on record at the National Archives seem trivial in comparison. For example, in the mid-1870s, a great cloud of grasshoppers devoured Nebraska's wheat fields.

In response, Congress passed the Nebraska Grasshopper Relief Act, which gave financial aid to farmers affected by the insect invasion. The grasshopper measure is hardly relevant to modern Americans, but it is still an important source for agricultural research.

Decisions made by the Supreme Court also have molded the course of U.S. history. In the *Dred Scott* decision (1857), the U.S. Supreme Court, dominated by southerners, declared that African-American slaves were not true citizens and therefore could be treated as property. The Dred Scott case infuriated northerners and brought the country a step closer to civil war. Just under one hundred years later, the *Brown v. Board of Education of Topeka, Kansas*, decision (1954) banned racially separate schools. The original written records of both the *Brown* and the *Dred Scott* cases are available to researchers in NARA's libraries.

During times of national emergency, Americans listen intently to speeches made by their president. The nation faced such a crisis in 1933, when the Great Depression gripped the country. In that dark time, one in four workers was unemployed, and many families suffered extreme hunger. President Franklin Delano Roosevelt calmed the people by declaring, "We have nothing to fear but fear itself."

Nearly a decade later, on December 7, 1941, Americans were stunned and outraged by Japan's surprise attack on Pearl Harbor, Hawaii. Speaking before Congress, President Roosevelt called December 7 "a date which will live in **infamy**."

*During the Great Depression in the 1930s, President Franklin D. Roosevelt delivered several radio talks called "fireside chats." He used these addresses to calm citizens' fears and to regain their trust in the nation's banking system. Roosevelt's fireside chats, as well as many other important presidential speeches, are housed at the National Archives.*

These Roosevelt speeches and many more presidential addresses are housed at the National Archives. Roosevelt's original typewritten speech following the Pearl Harbor attack is scribbled over with his inked-in corrections. Such a document is fascinating to historians who struggle to pierce the mind of the president on the day he led the nation into World War II.

## A Presidential Goodbye

Richard Nixon (1913–1994) is the only American president in history to resign his office. Stored in the National Archives is Nixon's very brief resignation note, dated August 9, 1974. The note, which is addressed to the Secretary of State, reads as follows: "I hereby resign the Office of the President of the United States."

*There are many surprises in store for tourists at the National Archives— but get there early to avoid the lines!*

UNITED STATES

National Archives

← Exhibition Hall
Theater →
Offices →
Research Facilities →
♿ →

# Chapter Three

# Thrilling the Tourist

Every day at about 9:30 A.M., lines of tourists begin to form in front of the National Archives Rotunda, which houses Exhibit Hall. (Here is a hint to all tourists: Get there early and take a walk around the building before you join the lines.) The National Archives Building is a work of art, with graceful columns weighing 95 tons each. A grayish limestone makes up its **façade**. Simple, strong lines project a feeling of grace and

*The Department of Justice medallion is one of thirteen medallions pinned to the outside walls of the National Archives.*

## Bricks and Mortar

The site of the National Archives covers 4.68 acres (2 ha). The building stands seven stories high.

stability. Here is a building that has been admired through many generations.

Near the upper floors of the building, thirteen circular medallions are pinned to the outside walls like badges of honor. The medallions represent the House of Representatives, the Senate, ten executive departments, and the Seal of the United States. The Department of Justice medallion, 8 feet (2.4 m) in diameter, shows a stern-faced man holding two law books under his arm.

Several statues stand outside the building. Rising on a pediment on Constitution Avenue is *The Recorder of the Archives*, a stone figure seated on a throne. Near him are sculpted

**papyrus** plants, a reminder that the ancient Egyptians once made paper from papyrus. Along Pennsylvania Avenue is the pediment *Destiny*, held aloft by two eagles. Under the statue *The Future*, also on this side of the building, is a chiseled message that could serve as the motto for the National Archives: WHAT IS PAST IS **PROLOGUE**.

*The* Destiny *pediment faces Pennsylvania Avenue.*

### Thank You, Mr. Shakespeare

The words "what's past is prologue" are spoken in *The Tempest*, written by the great English playwright William Shakespeare (1564–1616). A prologue is the introduction to a play. Thus, WHAT IS PAST IS PROLOGUE contains a special meaning: If you wish to gather an idea of possible future events, you must study past events.

# Welcome to Exhibit Hall

Visitors must join the lines at Constitution Avenue to enter Exhibit Hall, also called the Rotunda. The lines can be long. Visitors are required to check any large bags and to walk through a metal detector. Visitors to Exhibit Hall may take pictures, but not with a flash camera. As is true with sunlight, camera flashes tend to fade printing on old manuscripts.

The three Charters of Freedom—the Declaration of Independence, the Constitution, and the Bill of Rights—stand at the far end of Exhibit Hall. Situated between two mighty columns, the charters look as if they form the altar of a church. No one can take more than a couple of minutes to examine the charters because the viewing lines tend to be very long.

The three charters were written on **parchment**, which is made from sheepskin. In 1951, these fine parchments were carefully placed in a bulletproof glass frame filled with helium. Sealed in this manner, the Charters of Freedom

*Opposite: Tourists form a long line to view the Charters of Freedom in Exhibit Hall.*

**Rotunda Renovations**

Exhibit Hall at the National Archives Building was closed for major renovations during 2002.

Pictured here is a digital simulation of the new hall, which will be opened to the public in 2003.

were protected from outside air and dust. The documents are now preserved in specially designed containers made of pure titanium and filled with an inert gas called **argon**. Scientists believe the parchments will last hundreds of years and suffer no further deterioration. Ultraviolet light filters prevent the words from fading and give the charters a greenish haze.

At the touch of a button, the frames holding the Charters of Freedom can be lowered into a sealed 65-ton vault that lies 20 feet (6 m) below the floor. This lowering is done routinely

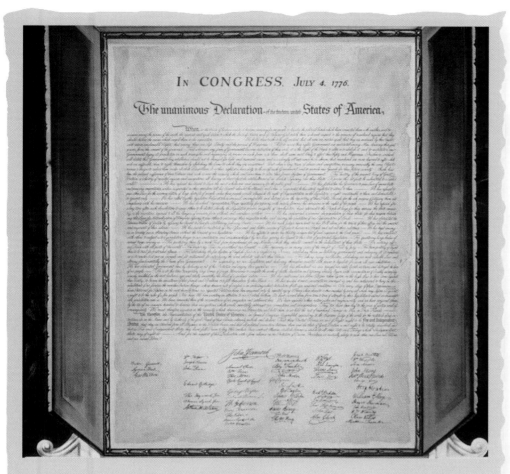

## Sign Your John Hancock

Despite the fading, it is still possible to see John Hancock's signature on the Declaration of Independence. Hancock (1737–1793) of Massachusetts was the first colonial leader to write his name on the declaration, and his signature is at least twice as large as the others. Generations of Americans grew up with the belief that Hancock made his signature particularly large as an act of rebellion. It was said he wanted England's King George III to read his signature without the aid of his spectacles. Many historians now claim this is a myth, however. Hancock's signature is on dozens of other items in the National Archives, and it seems he always signed official papers in a larger-than-life fashion.

*The Magna Carta on display at the National Archives was created in 1297.*

every night, but a guard can activate the system at any time in case of emergency.

Not to be missed in Exhibit Hall is one of NARA's oldest manuscripts: the Magna Carta. This document dates back to 1215, when a group of noblemen forced King John of England to sign a charter (called a *carta* in Latin) guaranteeing them certain rights. The Magna Carta enacted the first restrictions ever imposed on the power of an English king. The Magna Carta on display in Exhibit Hall was created in 1297. It is one of only four copies known to exist.

Besides being a destination for tourists, the National Archives serves as an active research center for scholars around the world. In this picture, researchers go about their business in the reading room.

# Chapter Four

# Serving the Researcher

Historian David McCullough, who has written many best-selling books on American history, conducts much of his research at the National Archives. In the introduction to Herman Viola's book *The National Archives of the United States*, McCullough calls the archives "one of the wonders of our country; the richest, most enthralling documentation we have as a nation, of who we are, what we have achieved, and what we stand for." McCullough is one of thousands of historians who probe through the National Archives seeking key items that will shed light on a chapter of the past. For them, writing history is similar to laboring over a jigsaw puzzle. One hard-to-find piece will often lead to a complete picture.

## The Thrill of Discovery

One need not be a professional historian who regularly publishes books to use the facilities of the National Archives. Anyone over fourteen who has a photo identification card is welcome. High-school students working on history projects often come to the National Archives to do research. The staff cautions students, however, that there are no history textbooks at the archives. The institution only handles primary, or original, sources—the foundations on which textbooks are written. A trip to the National Archives should be a researcher's last step after deciding which documents will be helpful. It should not be the first step.

To touch valuable and rare manuscripts requires special permission. The few visitors who are allowed to touch certain old documents must wear gloves. This "hands-on" experience adds to a historian's thrill of discovery. McCullough once wrote a book on the building of the Panama Canal. As a professional historian, he was allowed to touch the original treaty that permitted the United States to begin building the canal some one hundred years ago. "I felt a direct personal contact with that distant turning point," says McCullough of his research.

The National Archives is a storehouse of historical information, including old newspapers, census figures, and military records. To save space, archives staff have put much of this material on microfilm, which researchers string into a projector and read from a screen. Reading microfilm with a machine can be a clumsy process, but staff are always there to help.

*This archivist wears white gloves as he carefully examines original documents.*

Even with microfilm, the National Archives Building became much too crowded. By the late 1960s, the facility was overflowing with books, records, photos, and other artifacts. Clearly the National Archives needed to expand, so another facility was constructed in nearby College Park, Maryland, only 20 minutes away from downtown Washington. Opened in 1994, the six-story College Park building can serve up to 390 researchers at a time. Motion pictures, photographs,

*A 1989 photograph reveals the overcrowded state of the main National Archives Building.*

sound recordings, maps, and thousands of other museum pieces are held at College Park.

## Beyond Documents

Just about every paper written by the United States government in the last two hundred-plus years is stored at the National Archives. History is far more than words on paper, however. It is the saga of everyday people and the objects they cherished—photographs, trinkets, drawings, and more. Many

*The National Archives facility at College Park, Maryland, was opened in 1994.*

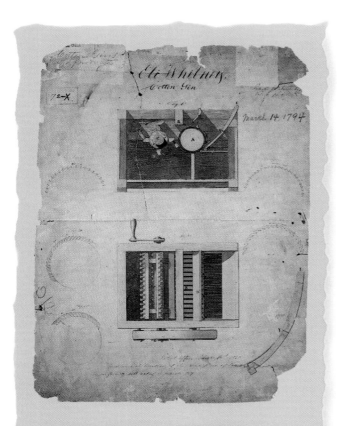

## Great and Not-So-Great Ideas

Great inventions change history. In 1793, Eli Whitney invented a simple machine, the cotton gin, which allowed one worker to clean raw cotton as fast as fifty workers could before. Whitney's patent, as well as his original drawings for the cotton gin (pictured above), are stored in the National Archives. The building also holds patents for Thomas Edison's light bulb, Samuel Colt's pistol, and Elisha Otis's elevator. One patent that failed to change history was one given in the 1800s for a piano that converted to a bed at night. Not all inventions are earth-shaking.

of these items, which are vital to the American memory, are held at the National Archives.

When Revolutionary War veterans applied for pensions, they had to prove their service in the Army or Navy. To furnish proof, many of them sent in their uniform buttons or the medals they won for valor. These tokens of the War of Independence eventually made their way to the National Archives, where they remain to this day.

Plans for machines and gadgets are also stored at the National Archives. When people invent a mechanical device, they apply for a patent at the U.S. Patent Office. Over the years, drawings and models of thousands of ingenious—and bizarre—devices were transferred from the Patent Office to the archives.

During World War I and World War II, the U.S. government produced posters that urged factory workers to toil harder for victory. The posters' powerful artwork warned of the dire consequences if the enemy won the war.

*This poster is one of many war propaganda pieces on file at the National Archives. Such idealized artwork was meant to gather support for the U.S. Armed Forces—and to inspire hatred for the enemy.*

The enemy also made skillful use of **propaganda**. During World War II, the Japanese government employed a young woman to demoralize American servicemen through radio

*In this Civil War photograph by Mathew Brady, a soldier offers a drink of water to his wounded companion. Brady took this picture after the Battle of Chancellorsville in early May 1863.*

broadcasts aimed at army camps. In reality, the soldiers enjoyed her programs because they included the latest music from home. The taped radio programs of "Tokyo Rose," as American soldiers called her, can be heard at listening rooms in the National Archives. Today, these items of propaganda help researchers to gauge the frenzy of life during wartime.

## "Smile, Mr. President"

The first U.S. president to be captured on film was Andrew Jackson, who posed before a camera in 1845. The original Jackson photo, as well as still pictures of every president since Jackson's time in office, are kept in the National Archives.

The National Archives also holds photographs and moving pictures that provide thrilling accounts of American history. One highlight is the series of haunting Civil War photos taken by pioneer cameraman Mathew Brady. Brady traveled from battlefield to battlefield and took more than 3,500 photos of wartime scenes.

Many researchers go to the National Archives to reconstruct their family history. The practice of filling out one's family tree is called genealogy.

FAMILY-REGISTER,
of Mr Nathaniel & Mrs. Mary Bangs.
Mr. Bangs was born October 2, 1760.
Mrs. Bangs was born March 26, 1763.
Were Married January 23, 1783.
By the Revd Josiah Deany of Berry.

| Two Children, viz. | Born. | Died. |
|---|---|---|
| Isaac H. Bangs | Nov. 23, 1783. | |
| A Son | Aug. 6, 1785 | Aug. 6, 1785. |

## Mrs. Bangs Died June 29, 1786.

Mr. Bangs was married (by the Revd David Parsons of Amherst) to Miss Electa Kellog his 2d Wife Jany 15, 1789. She was born August 6, 1764.

| Children's names. | Born. | Died. |
|---|---|---|
| A Daughter | March 12, 1790. | March 12, 1790. |
| Mary | May 21, 1791. | |
| Adolphus | Sep. 21, 1792. | |
| Sarah | June 8, 1794. | |
| Electa | Dec. 6, 1795. | |
| Nathaniel jr. | July 15, 1797. | Nov. 21, 1821. |
| Joel | Aug. 23, 1802. | |

Mr. Bangs                                    Mrs. Bangs

# Chapter Five

# Discovering Your Roots

About 70 percent of the researchers who come to the National Archives are working on the history of their own families. The practice of tracing one's family tree is called **genealogy**. People study their family histories for many reasons. Some hope to find a king, queen, or famous person in their **lineage**. Others probe into family history for practical purposes, such as settling a deceased relative's will. Genealogy has fascinated people for thousands of years.

## Working for History's Sake

The staff at the National Archives includes paid employees as well as many volunteers. By and large, they are people who are excited about the past. The National Archives staff, along with the people they assist, feel a thrill of discovery when they uncover just one piece of a family's history. Because many of the staff have researched their own family, they can provide vital tips to someone beginning his or her own genealogical quest.

The National Archives contains many records helpful to a person writing his or her family history. Staff can help both the experienced and the amateur genealogist to plug in missing information. Staff members urge family researchers to do a thorough background study before contacting the archives, however.

The best place to start writing a family history is at home. Think of yourself as a twig on the family tree. Start with what is known—your immediate relatives—and work from there. If possible, talk to your grandparents and find out where their grandparents lived. Get complete names, birthdates, and birthplaces if you can. What church did your relatives attend? Some churches have baptismal records going back hundreds of years. What holidays did your relatives celebrate? What type of work did they do? All of this is essential homework to complete before drawing up a family tree.

The National Archives keeps no birth records. It cannot answer the question, "What do you have on Mary Hogan, born May 10, 1901, in Philadelphia?" That question should be addressed to the Philadelphia City Hall. Records regarding births and deaths are kept at city, town, or county offices.

# Digging for Your Roots at the National Archives

Among NARA's most important genealogical tools are census records, military records, lists of ships' passengers, and documents concerning land transactions. With so much information to look through, it is helpful to come prepared. For example, know at least the approximate time your pioneer family lived outside of Independence, Missouri. Try to determine the year your great-grandfather was discharged from the Army after World War I. It helps tremendously to have a reference point—a date or a place—before probing the mountains of data available at the National Archives.

By law, the United States conducts a census, or head count,

every ten years. At one time census questionnaires were directed to the male head of the household, who was required to list the birthdates and birthplaces of all his children. With these records, a genealogist can track down a great- or even great-great-grandmother. Census records dating back to 1790 are kept at the National Archives Building. In order to protect individual privacy, however, personal census information is kept secret for seventy-two years. Thus, the 1930 census records were made public for the first time in 2002.

Suppose you have a distant uncle who was in the Union Army during the Civil War. Chances are that your uncle's military history will be at the National Archives, because NARA keeps records of all men and women who served in the federal forces from 1775 to 1902. A lucky researcher might find letters that a Civil War veteran wrote to his family. For example, one historian uncovered ten letters from nineteen-year-old Benjamin Chase of New Hampshire. The young soldier assured his father that he was not wasting his army pay of $13 a month: "i dont buy eny of the foolish stuff. You may think i do but i certain dont."

Perhaps your family originated in Europe or some other foreign land and immigrated to the United States within the last hundred years. The National Archives has records listing immigrants who arrived between 1790 and 1950. Again, do your homework before you tackle the problem of looking up your long-lost immigrant ancestor. Know the year he or she arrived, and, if you can, find out the name of the ship.

The National Archives' files of land deeds also contain valuable information for a genealogical search. Just about

## Roots

As a child, African-American writer Alex Haley (1921–1992) listened spell-bound as his older relatives told stories about his family. Often they spoke of the person who went back furthest in the family tree, a man known only as "the African." Haley was gripped with the idea of writing his family history. Material from the National Archives provided the foundation for the project, which led Haley on a trip to Africa. The result was his powerful 1976 book *Roots: The Saga of an American Family.* In 1977, the book became an eight-part series on television. The last episode was one of the most-watched events in television history.

everyone who applied for free land from the federal government under the Homestead Act and other land programs is on record at the archives. The files often include the names and birthdates of the applicants' children.

African-American genealogists often have difficulty tracing their distant ancestors. Slaves were bought and sold at the whim of their owners with little more notation than the slave's first name. In 1865, Congress established the Freedmen's Bureau to help liberated slaves adjust to a new life. Records of the Freedmen's Bureau, which operated until 1872, are kept at the National Archives and are invaluable to African-American genealogists.

The National Archives continues to carry out its function to preserve historical treasures and to aid the researcher. The building is a "must" place to visit for any visitor to Washington, D.C. The National Archives is America's memory. It is the root of the nation's family tree.

# Timeline

| | |
|---|---|
| **1774** | Charles Thomson is made secretary of the Continental Congress. |
| **1895** | J. Franklin Jameson begins his campaign to establish a national archives facility. |
| **1921** | A disastrous fire in Washington's Commerce Department Building destroys many records, including the 1890 census reports. |
| **1934** | The National Archives Establishment becomes an official agency of the U.S. government. |
| **1935** | The National Archives Building in Washington, D.C., is completed. |
| **1949** | The National Archives and Records Administration is established. |
| **1951** | The Charters of Freedom (the Declaration of Independence, the Constitution, and the Bill of Rights) are placed in helium-filled glass frames to prevent their further deterioration. |
| **1984** | The National Archives and Records Administration (NARA) is formed. |
| **1994** | A second National Archives Building is opened in College Park, Maryland. |

# Glossary

**advocate**—a person who supports or defends another person or a cause

**amendment**—a change or addition to a legal document

**Americana**—objects or lore pertaining to U.S. history

**argon**—a colorless, odorless gas

**confederation**—a political union composed of several self-governing states

**Corinthian**—following an architectural style inspired by the ancient Greek region of Corinth

**façade**—the outer, often decorative, face of a building

**genealogy**—the study of family history

**infamy**—an evil reputation brought about by a horrible deed or event

**lineage**—one's descendants or chain of ancestors

**memorabilia**—objects that stir memories

**papyrus**—a paper made from plants that was used in ancient Egypt

**parchment**—a writing surface made from animal skins

**pilings**—large wooden poles used in construction

**prologue**—lines introducing a play or novel

**propaganda**—boastful, often false statements designed to fire up emotions, often during wartime

# To Find Out More

## Books

Bober, Natalie. *Thomas Jefferson: Man on a Mountain*. New York: Aladdin Paperbacks, 1997.

Burgeson, Nancy. *My Family History*. Mahwah, NJ: Troll Associates, 1993.

Haley, Alex. *Roots*. New York: Dell Books, 1980.

Perl, Lila. *The Great Ancestor Hunt*. New York: Scott Foresman, 1990.

Pflueger, Lynda. *Mathew Brady: Photographer of the Civil War*. Berkeley Heights, NJ: Enslow Publishers, 2001.

# Organizations and Online Sites

National Archives and Records Administration
700 Pennsylvania Avenue NW
Washington, D.C. 20408
*http://www.nara.gov*

# A Note on Sources

To prepare for this book I went to Washington, D.C., and visited the National Archives Building several times. I had delightful talks with members of the NARA staff. The visit and the discussions were my most helpful sources when I finally sat down to write. Also important was studying many of the agency's official pamphlets, including "Using Records in the National Archives for Genealogical Research." Reading that pamphlet put me in the position of a young person starting out on the daunting task of tracing his or her family tree. I found an excellent book in Herman J. Viola's *The National Archives of the United States*, published in 1984. For inspiration I reread Alex Haley's 1977 book *Roots: The Saga of an American Family*. Haley did most of his research for *Roots* at the National Archives and claimed that material at the agency was vital for his project.

—*R. Conrad Stein*

# Index

Numbers in *italics* indicate illustrations.

# About the Author

R. Conrad Stein was born in Chicago. At age eighteen he enlisted in the Marines and served for three years. After discharge he attended the University of Illinois, where he graduated with a degree in history. He later earned an advanced degree at the University of Guanajuato in Mexico. Stein is a full-time writer of books for young readers. Over the years, he has published more than one hundred titles. Stein lives in Chicago with his wife, Deborah Kent, who is also an author of books for young readers, and their daughter, Janna.

027.5     Stein, R. Conrad
STE       The National Archives

| 9/03 | **DATE DUE** | | |
|---|---|---|---|
| | | | |
| | | | |
| | | | |
| | | | |
| | | | |
| | | | |
| | | | |
| | | | |
| | | | |
| | | | |
| | | | |
| | | | |